The Split History of the

D-DAY INVASION

GERMAN PERSPECTIVE

BY MICHAEL BURGAN

CONTENT CONSULTANT:
G. Kurt Piehler, PhD
Associate Professor of History
Director, Institute on World War and the Human Experience
Florida State University

COMPASS POINT BOOKS
a capstone imprint

About the Author

Michael Burgan is the author of more than 250 books for children and young adults, both fiction and nonfiction. His works include biographies of U.S. and world leaders and histories of the American Revolution, World War II, and the Cold War. He lives in Santa Fe, New Mexico, with his cat Callie.

Source Notes

Allies' Perspective:

Page 9, line 6: Dwight D. Eisenhower, *Report by the Supreme Commander to the Combined Chiefs of Staff on the Operations in Europe of the Allied Expeditionary Force, 6 June 1944 to 8 May 1945.* Washington, D.C.: Center of Military History, United States Army, 1994, p. v.

Page 10, line 15: Dwight D. Eisenhower, *Crusade in Europe.* Garden City, NY: Doubleday, 1948, p. 249.

Page 15, line 4: Jon E. Lewis, ed. *D-Day As They Saw It.* New York: Carroll & Graf, 2004, p. 63.

Page 15, line 8: Ibid., p. 61.

Page 18, line 19: Marcelle Hamel-Hateau, "Army of Shadows," *Harper's Magazine,* June 2014. 23 Oct. 2017. https://harpers.org/archive/2014/06/army-of-shadows

Page 19, line 15: *D-Day As They Saw It,* p. 98.

Page 21, line 4: Ibid., p. 103.

Page 22, line 14: Ibid., p. 129.

Page 22, line 20: Scott Simon, "The Speech Eisenhower Never Gave On The Normandy Invasion," NPR.org, 8 June 2013. 23 Oct. 2017. http://www.npr.org/2013/06/08/189535104/the-speech-eisenhower-never-gave-on-the-normandy-invasion

Page 22, line 24: Richard Preston and Ben Hazell, "D-Day: June 6th 1944 As It Happened," *The Telegraph,* 6 June 2014. 23 Oct. 2017. http://www.telegraph.co.uk/history/world-war-two/10878674/D-Day-6th-June-1944-as-it-happened-live.html

Page 26, line 14: *Crusade in Europe,* p. 280.

Page 26, line 15: Ibid., p. 280.

Page 29, line 18: *Report by the Supreme Commander . . .,* p. 122.

German Perspective:

Page 5, line 10: *D-Day As They Saw It,* p. 92.

Page 5, line 11: Ibid., p. 92.

Page 5, line 15: Werner Kortenhaus, "I Saw British Bombs and Knew It Was War," *BBC News,* 1 June 2004. 23 Oct. 2017. http://thewe.cc/contents/more/archive2004/june/i_saw_the_british_bombs.htm

Page 8, line 7: Richard Hargreaves. *The Germans in Normandy.* Mechanicsburg, Pa.: Stackpole Books, 2008, p. 6.

Page 10, line 5: B.H. Liddell-Hart, ed., *The Rommel Papers.* Translated by Paul Findlay. London: Collins Clear-Type Press, 1953, p. 455.

Page 12, line 3: Cornelius Ryan, *The Longest Day: June 6, 1944.* New York: Simon and Schuster, 1994, p. 27.

Page 16, line 20: *The Germans in Normandy,* p. 17.

Page 16, line 24: *The Rommel Papers,* p. 464.

Page 20, line 14: *The Longest Day: June 6, 1944,* p. 100.

Page 22, line 9: "'Beast of Omaha' Weeps as He Recalls Slaughter of Thousands on Beach," *The Scotsman,* 6 June 2004. 23 Oct. 2017. http://www.scotsman.com/news/world/beast-of-omaha-weeps-as-he-recalls-slaughter-of-thousands-on-beach-1-1394712

Page 25, line 5: *The Germans in Normandy,* pp. 65–66.

Page 26, line 10: Ibid., p. 81.

Page 27, line 23: Ibid., p. 237.

Page 28, line 16: Ian Kershaw, *Hitler: A Biography.* New York: W. W. Norton & Co., 2008, p. 875.

Table of Contents

SHARED RESOURCES

CHAPTER 1 DEFENDING OCCUPIED LANDS

On the night of June 5, 1944, Werner Kortenhaus was on patrol with several other men from Germany's 21st Panzer Division. Just after midnight, Kortenhaus heard enemy aircraft fly overhead. It was a common sound to the Germans as they were often the target of enemy bombs. But these planes weren't on a bombing run—they were flying too low for that. The German soldiers guessed that the planes might be dropping supplies to the French Resistance. But they didn't see anything, so they returned to their camp north of Falaise, France.

Just weeks before, 19-year-old Kortenhaus and his division had moved to Falaise from Brittany, a region farther west along the northern coast of France. Their commander, General Erwin Rommel, was in charge of defending the coast against an amphibious assault from the Allies.

Back at camp, Kortenhaus saw the men in his unit standing by their tanks. It was after midnight, and most of the men should have been asleep. He learned that Allied paratroopers had landed near the city of Caen. By 2 a.m. the division was ready to go, but hours passed before the tanks began to move. "[We] just stood there, inactive by our tanks," Kortenhaus later recalled. "We couldn't understand why we weren't getting any orders. . . . " Finally, at 8 a.m. the division rolled toward Caen. In the distance, Kortenhaus could see smoke over the city from enemy bombs. He thought to himself, "My God, this is war."

a German Panzer division

GERMANY ATTACKS EUROPE

German Chancellor Adolf Hitler had started World War II (1939–1945) by invading Poland. Then he set his sights on Western Europe. Italy sided with Germany in the fight. Those two countries, along with Japan, formed the Axis Powers. Japan supported Germany's desire to take over most of Europe, while Germany supported Japan's efforts to control large parts of Asia. By 1941 Germany had conquered 11 European countries.

Hitler had risen to power in 1933 by reminding Germans how badly they were treated after losing World War I (1914–1918). The victorious nations, which included Great Britain, France, and the United States, had forced Germany to dismantle its military

Adolf Hitler salutes his Nazi troops as they march through Poland in 1939.

and give up lands it controlled in Europe. Hitler wanted to take back those lost lands and conquer new lands as well. He considered the Germans a "master race" that should rule over people he thought were inferior, such as Polish people and Russians.

As he gained political power, Hitler blamed Jewish people for many of Germany's problems. Once his Nazi Party took control of the government, Hitler began taking away the rights of German Jews and sent many of them to prisons called concentration camps. When World War II began, Germany also built death camps designed to kill large numbers of Jews and other people that Hitler considered a threat to Germany. By the end of the war, more than 6 million people perished in those camps.

In June 1941 Hitler went after his biggest military target yet—the Soviet Union. He sent about 3 million men and almost 4,000 tanks to the battlefront, which stretched for 1,000 miles (1,609 kilometers) along the Soviet border. At first, the Germans advanced quickly as they had in Western Europe. But the Soviet defenses improved. They stopped the German advance, and in 1943 the Soviets began to push them back. Along this Eastern Front, Germany suffered heavy losses. Going into June 1944, the Germans had suffered almost 5 million casualties, including more than 1 million killed. But that didn't stop Hitler from wanting to keep fighting the Soviets.

BUILDING THE WALL

After switching his attention to the Eastern Front in June 1941, Hitler left the Atlantic coast lightly defended. But when the United States entered the war in December, Hitler realized that the Allies would likely open a second battlefront along the Atlantic coast. This would force him to move troops from the east to defend France.

In the spring of 1942, Hitler announced his plan to build a line of defenses that would stretch along the Atlantic coast from Norway to southern France. This "Atlantic Wall" would be comprised of 15,000 well-protected bunkers and other defensive positions, most of them in France. Hitler told some of his military officers, "I will not give up one foot of ground which is soaked in the blood of German soldiers."

About 5,000 fortifications already existed along the coast when Hitler ordered the building of the Atlantic Wall. He wanted the wall completed by May 1943, which seemed like an impossible task. Still, 260,000 men began the work—including French citizens and other non-Germans who were forced to work for the Nazis.

One German officer did not think much of the wall. General Gerd von Rundstedt commanded Nazi troops in France and other parts of Western Europe. He doubted the wall would slow down an invading army for more than a day. Many of von Rundstedt's troops were worn out from fighting the Soviets. Others were teenagers who had just joined the *Wehrmacht,* the German Army. Many of the troops in German uniforms were actually foreigners. Some of them volunteered, but many were prisoners of war forced to fight for Germany.

Von Rundstedt had another problem. While his official title was "supreme commander," he couldn't make decisions regarding the troops. He had to follow Hitler's orders. The general once bitterly joked that he could not move a single soldier without first getting Hitler's permission.

ROMMEL ARRIVES

In the fall of 1943, with the Atlantic Wall far from complete, Hitler decided to send General Erwin Rommel to the Atlantic coast to gauge what still needed to be done. Rommel held the rank of field marshal, the highest level of general in the Wehrmacht. From February 1941 to March 1943, Rommel led the German forces fighting in North Africa. His success there earned him the nickname, "the Desert Fox."

When he began his inspection of the Atlantic Wall, Rommel was not impressed with it. He focused his attention on France because he assumed the Allies would attack there. To Rommel, the German strategy should be to wipe out the enemy before they even reached the beach or just as they came ashore. The goal was to stop the Allies from gaining a beachhead. Rommel was sure he could do the job.

General Erwin Rommel (third from left) leads an inspection of the Atlantic Wall.

On December 31, 1943, Rommel sent a note to Hitler describing his thoughts on how the Allies might attack and the defenses the Germans would need. From his previous military experience, Rommel knew the value of land mines. He proposed building "a fortified and mined zone extending from the coast some 5 or 6 miles [8 or 10 km] inland and defended both to the sea and to the land." The current land mines in place, he wrote, would not do the job. Rommel had other thoughts on the kinds of weapons the defenders would need—particularly anti-tank and antiaircraft weapons and machine guns. He also thought Panzer divisions and other troops should be moved closer to the coast so they could attack if the Allies did make it through the coastal defenses.

Hitler decided to put Rommel in charge of part of the German military called Army Group B. Made up of two smaller armies—the Seventh and the Fifteenth—Army Group B was the strongest German force in western Europe. This change meant that Rommel ranked below von Rundstedt, but he had great freedom to put his thoughts into action. His job was to prepare the German defenses in France as best he could, as quickly as possible.

Resistance Nests

Part of the German defenses along the French coast were *widerstandsnests* (WNs) or "resistance nests." Many were just trenches dug in the ground with tunnels that connected them to other nests nearby. The best of the resistance nests offered more protection. They were actual bunkers with ceilings made of concrete more than 6 feet (1.8 meters) thick. Some nests could hold up to 30 men and guns of various sizes. The men fired their guns through openings in the walls.

One resistance nest along the coast of Normandy, WN 62, held 20 men and had four machine guns and three larger guns. Land mines and barbed wire protected the nests. In some places, deep trenches meant to stop advancing enemy tanks ran between two nests. Despite their best efforts, soldiers stationed at WNs in Normandy faced fierce fighting when the Allies attacked.

Cannons from German resistance nests were aimed toward the English Channel to prevent the enemy from landing on the beaches of Normandy.

CHAPTER 2

PREPARING FOR THE INVASION

With his new orders to improve the Atlantic Wall, Rommel went to work. To him, defeating the Allies on the beaches was the key to his mission. He told an aide, "We'll have only one chance to stop the enemy and that's while he's in the water . . . struggling to get ashore." The first 24 hours of fighting, Rommel predicted, would decide who would control France. He was right.

Rommel's plan included strengthening the current defensive positions and building new ones, as Hitler had ordered. Rommel also wanted a second line of defensive posts away from the coast, even though he held to his belief that the enemy had to be defeated at the shore. He believed this, in part, because the German air force, known as the *Luftwaffe,* was so weak. The Luftwaffe had already lost many of its best pilots in the fighting, and it didn't have long-range reconnaissance planes that could provide detailed intelligence on the Allies' movements. Although Germany had many large industries, it could not quickly produce new planes, tanks, and other weapons like the Allies could. For those reasons, Rommel could not count on the Luftwaffe to stop the Allies from bringing men and supplies ashore if they established a beachhead.

Land mines were a huge part of Rommel's defensive buildup. Early in 1944, he ordered 20 million new land mines placed along the coast of France and farther inland. His defensive buildup also extended into the water. In the spring of 1944, the Germans began building four lines of obstacles in the water. These included 10-foot

Obstacles like these lined the beaches and the shallow waters along the Normandy coast.

(3-m) sections of iron fencing known as Belgian gates and steel obstacles called hedgehogs. The hedgehogs had sharp points that could rip open the bottom of the Allies' landing craft. Rommel assumed the Allies would attack at high tide and would not see most of the obstacles, which were visible only at low tide.

Rommel thought deception was key too. The Germans built fake artillery positions hoping that the Allies would waste time and ammunition attacking them instead of the actual positions. Some of the real guns were hidden under netting covered with branches.

Rommel ordered his men to dam up rivers or cut paths so seawater would pour in. If the Allies got past the shore, this flooding would make it difficult for them to move farther inland. Rommel also had his men cut down trees to use as obstacles and destroy coastal homes to give gunners a clear view.

A Deadly Spear

Rommel actually designed some of the obstacles that his men set up along the French coast. One, nicknamed "Rommel's asparagus," consisted of 10-foot (3-m) tall wooden posts and concrete poles driven into the ground with explosives on top. They were connected to wires that, when hit by glider planes or paratroopers, set off the explosives. In tests, gliders that flew too close to the poles were heavily damaged. But the Allied attack came before Rommel's men could equip all the poles with explosives. And on D-Day, the Allies managed to avoid most of the asparagus and landed safely.

DIFFERING VIEWS

Some of the major work to strengthen the Atlantic Wall took place near Pas-de-Calais. Hitler was convinced the Allied attack would come there because it marked the shortest distance between England and France across the English Channel. Rommel's Fifteenth Army was based near there. The smaller Seventh Army defended the southern part of Normandy. Over time, Rommel disagreed with Hitler and other generals on where the Allies might land. He knew Pas-de-Calais was the likely target. But Rommel began to wonder if the Allies might land where the Germans didn't expect them. He thought one possible location was the beaches of Normandy.

Rommel also had his disagreements with von Rundstedt, who believed the best strategy was to let the Allies come ashore and then counterattack with the German tank divisions. His thought was that the guns on the Allied ships in the English Channel would not be able to reach the tanks. The tanks closest to the coast were under the command of General Leo Geyr von Schweppenburg, and he shared von Rundstedt's view. But knowing the strength of the Allied air force, Rommel thought the German tanks would be easy targets. Hitler supported Rommel when it came to building up the coastal defenses, but he did not give Rommel command over all the tanks he wanted. From the start, Hitler had asserted control over many details of the war in Europe, including ordering tanks into battle.

Hitler and Rommel disagreed on vehicles too. Rommel's infantry did not have enough vehicles to move the men and their supplies where they were needed. Many of the soldiers had to rely on carts pulled by horses and donkeys, and even those were sometimes in short supply. When Rommel asked for more vehicles, Hitler said troops should stand and fight. But even if Hitler wanted to give Rommel more vehicles, Germany was unable to provide enough to both the Eastern Front and the troops in the west. In France, the Germans had to rely on trains to move men and supplies. But that proved more and more difficult as the Allies increased their bombing raids on railways.

THE GERMANS' WEAPONS AND MEN

Starting in the fall of 1943, Germany also moved thousands more troops into France. Many were young and had never fought before. The new recruits included thousands of members of the Hitler Youth. The Nazi Party had created this organization even before it took power in 1933. Millions of young Germans eventually joined. They learned Hitler's beliefs that Germans were superior to others and that Germans must be ready to sacrifice for their country. They pledged their loyalty to Hitler and were ready to do whatever he demanded. In the Wehrmacht, the Hitler Youth committed to fighting for Germany until death. Jochen Leykauff was one young German ready for battle. He said, "We were not afraid."

Although Rommel did not get everything he wanted, during the spring of 1944 the Germans greatly strengthened their defenses in France. This seemed to bring Rommel added confidence. In May, he wrote his wife, "It's quite amazing what has been achieved in the

Beginning in 1939 all non-Jewish boys and girls in Germany were required to join the Nazi youth program at age 10.

last few weeks. I'm convinced that the enemy will have a rough time of it when he attacks, and ultimately achieve no success."

Rommel and von Rundstedt both thought the Allied assault would come soon. Allied bombing raids had increased around Pas-de-Calais, suggesting that it was still the likely target. But they had no idea exactly when and where the invasion would come.

CHAPTER 3 THE ENEMY ARRIVES

On June 1 the Germans' intelligence team in France picked up the first half of a coded radio message sent to the French Resistance. They knew this was just a signal to alert the Resistance that a second message would soon follow. That second message would likely reveal when the invasion would begin.

Word reached one of Rommel's armies to be on alert. But his troops in Normandy did not receive the message. In any event, when Rommel received the weather forecast on June 4, he thought it would be too stormy for the Allies to risk coming ashore. He figured they would wait until later in the month when the tides would again be in their favor. With that belief, Rommel headed to Germany to meet with Hitler and see his wife on her birthday. The forecast also convinced General Friedrich Dollmann, who commanded Rommel's army in Normandy, that the attack would be delayed. Dollmann arranged for a training exercise to be held offsite on June 6 and ordered many top officers to attend.

THE PLOT AGAINST HITLER

In early June, after Rommel left for Germany, one of his officers held a small dinner party. The discussion focused on how to achieve peace in Europe—without Adolf Hitler. But getting rid of him would not be easy. One option was to work out a secret peace deal with the Allies and then force Hitler to stand trial. The other option was to kill Hitler. Although he wasn't there, Rommel knew of these plans. He wanted Hitler out of power too, but he didn't openly support killing him.

After D-Day, more German officers supported the effort to overthrow the Nazi government. They wanted to end a war they believed they could not win. On July 20, 1944, officers led by Colonel Claus von Stauffenburg attempted to kill Hitler with a small bomb hidden inside a briefcase. When the plot failed, many of those involved were caught and arrested. Even their family members were arrested. In all, more than 7,000 people were arrested and nearly 5,000 were killed or forced to commit suicide. Although Rommel was not directly involved in the plot, he was given a choice—face a trial and then be executed, or kill himself. On October 14, 1944, Rommel chose suicide.

On June 5 the weather also influenced the German Navy. Like the Luftwaffe, the German Navy was not the potent force it had once been. Its best weapon, submarines called U-boats, were most effective in deep ocean waters, but they were not as useful in the English Channel. Most of the ships available in France were small patrol boats or faster E-boats—tiny vessels that were good for attacking a few ships quickly and then speeding away. But they couldn't match the fleet of large, powerful ships the Allies had. The rough seas on June 5 forced most German boats to remain in their harbors.

THE FIRST ATTACKS

On the night of June 5, German intelligence received the second message meant to alert the French Resistance. Soon, a message went out to the German commanders across France: "Message of BBC . . . According to our available records it means 'Expect invasion within 48 hours, starting [midnight] June 6.'" For reasons unknown, this message also did not reach Rommel's army in Normandy.

Shortly after midnight on June 6, German troops began to see the first Allied paratroopers landing not far from the Normandy coast. In Saint-Lô, reports reached the headquarters of General Erich Marcks while he and some officers celebrated his birthday. One officer thought they might be supply troops for the French Resistance. But as more reports came in of paratroopers landing across the region, the officers realized that an attack was under way.

But they didn't know if this was the main invasion or just an attempt to confuse them. One thing added to the confusion—some of the paratroopers were dummies, not soldiers ready for battle.

General Marcks quickly told his men to prepare to fight, but other officers were slow to react. There had been false alarms before, so many officers wanted to be sure an invasion was really under way before taking action. When Major Werner Pluskat heard that paratroopers had been spotted, he went down to the beach to check. Looking out over the English Channel, he saw nothing, but he did hear more enemy planes overhead than usual.

By 3 a.m. Werner Kortenhaus' Panzer division was ready to roll. But the order to move didn't come. The officers who received reports of the Allied landings didn't call Rommel, who was then asleep at his home in Germany.

Thousands of Allied paratroopers landed in Normandy on D-Day.

FIGHTING ON THE BEACH

By 5 a.m. the movement of Allied ships and warplanes convinced General von Rundstedt that the invasion was real, even though he still expected the major invasion at Pas-de-Calais. But on the beaches of Normandy, Major Pluskat saw something that astonished him. Looking through binoculars, he saw an immense fleet coming right toward him. His men were already in their widerstandsnests, waiting for an attack.

In WN 62, Corporal Heinrich Severloh listened to instructions from his lieutenant: "You must open fire when the enemy is knee-deep in the water and is still unable to run quickly."

Across the beaches of Normandy, men in defensive positions waited for the Allies to come ashore. The Germans heard bombs exploding all around, but many of them missed their targets. At 6:30 a.m. the Allies began storming the beaches. From their defensive positions, the Germans fired artillery and machine guns. Soon the beaches were filled with dead and wounded soldiers.

WN 62 was positioned above the beach, so Corporal Severloh had an easy shot at the enemy. As each new wave of Allies hit the shore, he fired his machine gun. Before the morning was over, he alone had fired more than 10,000 bullets.

Throughout the morning, more Allies streamed ashore. Meanwhile, their ships in the channel fired large guns and hit many of the Germans' positions. Some Allied troops were able to attack the German artillery or bunkers directly, sometimes using grenades. German soldiers began to surrender rather than face certain death. Others were caught as they tried to flee.

As Allied troops stormed the beaches of Normandy, they had to dodge bullets fired from the Germans' defensive positions.

LATE DECISIONS

At Hitler's home in southern Germany, news of an attack came in around 5 a.m. But given the uncertainty of the news, no one told Hitler until later that morning. The top military commander there was General Alfred Jodl. He read the reports, but he wasn't convinced the invasion was real, so he denied an early request for reinforcements.

Hitler was a late sleeper, and no one dared wake him. When he finally woke and learned of the attack, he clung to his old belief that the real invasion was still to come at Pas-de-Calais. Soon after, around 10:15 a.m., Rommel got his first detailed report of the attack. By early afternoon he was speeding across Germany back to his headquarters in France.

Meanwhile, the 21st Panzer Division was on the move. Allied bombing had destroyed the city of Caen so badly that the tanks had to spend several hours going around it. That afternoon, commanders in the field learned that the reserve Panzer divisions that Hitler controlled would also be heading to the front. But they were even farther away and would not reach Normandy until the next day. In the hours since the invasion had begun, the Allies had landed on five different beaches. And they continued to bring in more men, tanks, and supplies.

When the tanks of the 21st Panzer Division finally reached Caen, the Allies were ready for them. After quickly losing 10 tanks, the Germans pulled back. As they continued to lose more tanks, word reached Rommel that the Allies were bringing ashore one tank every minute. Despite evidence to the contrary, Hitler was still convinced that the major attack was yet to come.

Chapter 4 The Direction of History

On June 7, the residents of Berlin learned of the enemy attack in France. A Nazi newspaper assured Germans that their troops were winning the battle—something none of their generals in Normandy believed. The paper went on to say that Hitler was their "guarantee of victory."

On that morning, German tanks began another counterattack near Caen. This time they were able to keep Allied forces from taking the city. Meanwhile, German fighter planes finally reached Normandy and began to attack the beaches. However, Allied fighter planes shot down most of them before they could reach the coast.

With the success of the Allied invasion, General von Rundstedt admitted that Rommel had been right—the Germans should have kept more tanks closer to Normandy. Rommel's prediction had also come true: The first 24 hours of the invasion had been crucial.

The Germans raced to bring tanks, soldiers, and supplies to this new battlefront. They fought back where they could, but their counterattacks did little to slow down the Allies. They had to concentrate on stopping the Allies from advancing and landing more troops. In addition, the Allies' air power slowed the advancement of German troops. One soldier described how Allied bombs "came whistling down . . . and men, weapons, and fragments of vehicles were thrown into the air." Even as they struggled, the German soldiers earned praise from both Rommel and von Rundstedt for their bravery.

The Secret Weapons

After D-Day the Germans introduced two new weapons. The V-1 was a pilotless plane that carried nearly a ton of explosives. It was designed to fly over the English Channel, crash-land on cities in England, and kill civilians. The first V-1 reached London on June 13, and many more followed. But eventually the British began shooting them down before they could reach their targets.

Germany's other secret weapon, the V-2 rocket, flew at speeds over 2,000 miles (3,219 km) per hour while carrying explosives. Unlike the V-1, the V-2 could not be shot down in flight. The first V-2s were launched in September 1944. Allied attacks made it difficult for the Germans to get fuel for their secret weapons, and ultimately, they did not help the Germans win the war.

A LOSING BATTLE

Ten days after the invasion began, Hitler met with Rommel and von Rundstedt. By then the Germans had suffered more than 25,000 casualties. Hitler promised that more weapons and men would be sent to Normandy, but he still expected another amphibious attack. Rommel left the meeting hopeful that the Germans could still win. But soldiers in the field couldn't see how they could win when the Allies completely controlled the skies over the battlefield.

One bright spot for the Germans came in July. Around Caen, the Germans stopped an Allied advance and destroyed 400 tanks. In early August the Allies actually had more casualties than the Germans, but the Allies could rush troops into battle faster than the Germans. By then Field Marshal Günther von Kluge had replaced von Rundstedt, who had become convinced that Germany could not win. Rommel was no longer in France either, after being wounded in mid-July.

In August a second Allied landing did come but not at Pas-de-Calais. Instead, Allied forces landed in the south of France and quickly pushed northward. In September the Germans were able to stop an invasion in the Netherlands, but the Allies had pushed eastward into Belgium and were closing in on the German border. German troops retreated quickly, sometimes leaving their vehicles behind when they ran out of fuel. Some faced angry French civilians, who wanted revenge after being under Nazi rule. One German soldier wrote in his diary, "There's machine-gun fire and rifle fire from rooftops, from cellars, from windows." Those who escaped the shooting struggled to find enough food to survive.

A LAST GASP

Despite his losses, Hitler still believed his forces could defeat the Allies. But he needed more troops, so the German government began calling up boys just 16 and 17 years old. The Hitler Youth also sought volunteers. In Germany civilians were given weapons and military training to prepare for an Allied invasion. Many of them were killed fighting in eastern Germany as Soviet troops advanced toward Berlin.

The Allies' rapid advance had one advantage for Germany. It was harder for the Allies to get supplies from Normandy's beaches to the front lines. At the same time, as German troops were pushed back toward their homeland, it was easier for them to get supplies. Germany also increased production of fighter planes, making almost 3,000 in September alone. But pilots and fuel were still in short supply.

Throughout the fall, Hitler made plans for one huge counterattack against the Allies on the Western Front. He called the plan Operation Autumn Mist. Hitler told an aide, "If it doesn't succeed, I see no other possibility of bringing the war to a favorable conclusion." Even so, in the orders he sent to his generals, he wrote that no one was to change any details of his plan.

By December the Allies were deep into Belgium and almost to Germany. On December 16 a German counterattack began in Belgium's Ardennes Forest. To prepare for the attack, the Germans had snuck some of their troops behind Allied lines. Using the uniforms and weapons of captured Americans, they cut telephone lines and performed other acts of sabotage. When the Allies learned that there were spies in their midst, they set up checkpoints and quizzed passersby on American pop culture. In one incident, American guards who thought they'd caught a spy, shot out the tires of the British Field Marshal's car.

At first the Ardennes move took the Allies by surprise, and for a week the Germans pushed them back. But by the end of 1944, the Allies had stopped the German advance. Going into the new year, the Allies began pushing eastward into Germany.

THE END

After the failure of Operation Autumn Mist, the German Army was doomed. Soviet troops moving in from the east were getting closer to Berlin, while the Allies moved in from the west. By mid-April 1945, Hitler was living full-time in a bunker in Berlin. By April 20 the Soviets had reached the heart of Berlin. Realizing that Germany had lost the war, Hitler killed himself on April 30. A week later, Germany surrendered.

Hitler's Atlantic Wall and Rommel's efforts could not stop the Allies from landing in Normandy. Bad intelligence and bad decisions played parts in that failure. Facing fighting on two fronts, Nazi Germany could not survive. With Hitler's defeat, the world learned about the horrors of the death camps. Although many inmates were freed when the Allies took control of the camps, millions of others had already perished inside. The surviving Nazi leaders faced a trial, and 12 were executed for their roles in setting up the camps or massacring other civilians. Ultimately, D-Day was the beginning of the end of Nazi Germany's control over much of Europe.

INDEX

Select Bibliography

Ambrose, Stephen E. *D-Day June 6, 1944: The Climactic Battle of World War II.* London: Pocket Books, 2002.

Eisenhower, Dwight D. *Crusade in Europe*. London: William Heinemann, 1948.

Hargreaves, Richard. *The Germans in Normandy.* Mechanicsburg, Pa.: Stackpole Books, 2008.

Hart, Russell A. *Clash of Arms: How the Allies Won in Normandy.* Boulder, Colo.: Lynne Rienner Publishers, 2001.

Lewis, Jon E., ed. *D-Day As They Saw It.* New York: Carroll & Graf, 2004.

Liddell-Hart, B.H., ed. *The Rommel Papers.* Translated by Paul Findlay. London: Collins Clear-Type Press, 1953.

Mayo, Jonathan. *D-Day: Minute by Minute.* New York: Marble Arch Press, 2014.

McManus, John C. *The Americans at D-Day: The American Experience at the Normandy Invasion.* New York: Macmillan, 2005.

Mitcham. Samuel W. *Rommel's Last Battle: The Desert Fox and the Normandy Campaign.* New York: Stein and Day, 1983.

Ryan, Cornelius. *The Longest Day: June 6, 1944.* New York: Simon and Schuster, 1994.

Wilt, Alan F. *The Atlantic Wall: Hitler's Defenses in the West, 1941–1944.* Ames, Iowa: The Iowa State University Press, 1975.

Further Reading

Atkinson, Rick. *D-Day: The Invasion of Normandy, 1944.* New York: Henry Holt and Company, 2014.

Burgan, Michael. *Turning Point: The Story of the D-Day Landings.* North Mankato, Minn.: Capstone Publishers, 2017.

Donohue, Moira Rose. *The Invasion of Normandy: Epic Battle of World War II.* Mankato, Minn.: North Star Editions, 2016.

Sepahban, Lois. *12 Incredible Facts About the D-Day Invasion.* North Mankato, Minn.: Peterson Publishing Company, 2016.

Critical Thinking Questions

1. What were some of the major advantages the Allies had before D-Day? What problems did the Germans face as they tried to prepare for the attack? Refer to the text and outside sources, as needed, to support your answer.
2. Why did you think some German soldiers remained so committed to their country's cause even as it became clear it would be almost impossible to win the war?
3. How important were intelligence and deception for the Allies? Give examples of how they helped the Allies accomplish their goals. Use evidence from the text to support your answer.

December 8: The United States and more than a dozen other countries declare war on Japan

December 11: Germany and Italy declare war on the United States

1942

March: Hitler announces plans to build the "Atlantic Wall," a line of defenses stretching along the Atlantic Coast from Norway to southern France

1944

Spring: In anticipation of an Allied invasion, the Germans begin planting mines and other obstacles along the Normandy coast

May: Eisenhower decides Operation Overlord (D-Day) will take place in early June

June 4: Due to the weather, Eisenhower postpones D-Day until June 6; seeing the forecast, Rommel assumes an attack will come later in the month; he heads to Germany, and General Dollmann orders officers to attend a training exercise on June 6

June 5: Eisenhower gives the OK for D-Day to take place the next day; ships filled with soldiers head across the English Channel toward France

August 15: The Allies launch a second amphibious assault, this time in southern France

August 25: After four years of occupation, Paris is liberated by Allied forces

September: American troops heading north from southern France meet up with Allied forces pushing east from Normandy; together they advance toward the German border

September 17: An Allied assault called Operation Market Garden begins in the Netherlands; after more than a week of fighting, the Germans push back the Allies

December 16: The Battle of the Bulge begins in Belgium's Ardennes Forest; during the three weeks the battle lasts, the Americans suffer more than 100,000 casualties

1945

April 20: Soviet troops begin bombing Berlin

April 30: Hitler commits suicide

May 8: Germany surrenders, ending the war in Europe

TIMELINE

1939

September 1: Germany invades Poland

September 3: Great Britain, France, Australia, and New Zealand declare war on Germany

1940

May 10: German troops invade the Netherlands, Belgium, and Luxembourg; all three countries surrender by the end of the month

May 12: Germany invades France

June 10: Italy declares war on Great Britain and France

June 22: France surrenders to Germany

1941

June 22: Germany invades and declares war on the Soviet Union

September: A German siege of the Russian city of Leningrad begins; by the time it ends in January 1944, more than 500,000 Russians starve to death

December 7: Japan attacks the U.S. naval base at Pearl Harbor, Hawaii

June 6, 12:00 a.m.: Commandos flying in lightweight glider planes land near Bénouville, France; they quickly take control of two key bridges; Jedburgh teams and paratroopers begin parachuting into France; German troops spot the paratroopers, but their generals are slow to react

June 6, 5:00 a.m.: News of a possible attack reaches Hitler's home in Germany, but no one tells him until he wakes up five hours later

June 6, 6:30 a.m.: American forces begin storming Omaha and Utah beaches on the Normandy coast

June 6, 7:30 a.m.: British forces invade Gold and Sword beaches

June 6, 8:00 a.m.: Canadian forces land at Juno Beach; by the end of the day, the Allies have brought more than 150,000 men ashore while suffering about 11,000 casualties

June 6, 10:00 a.m.: The British Broadcasting Company (BBC) plays a recorded message from Eisenhower announcing the Allied invasion on the Normandy coast in an attempt to liberate Europe

July 20: A group of German officers lead a failed attempt to kill Hitler

GLOSSARY

AMPHIBIOUS—able to operate in water and on land

ANTI-SEMITISM—prejudice or discrimination against Jewish people

BEACHHEAD—a place or position that serves as a base for an army

BUNKER—an underground shelter to protect from bomb attacks and gunfire

CASUALTIES—people killed, wounded, or missing in battle or war

COMMANDO—a soldier who makes quick, destructive raids on enemy territory

COUNTERATTACK—an assault launched after an enemy's opening attack

EASTERN FRONT—the course of World War II in Eastern Europe and Russia

FORTIFICATION—a building or wall built as a military defense

LIBERATION—the act of freeing a person, group, or nation

METEOROLOGIST—a person who studies and predicts the weather

MORTAR—a short cannon that fires shells or rockets high in the air

PARATROOPER—a soldier trained to jump by parachute into battle

RECONNAISSANCE—dealing with the military observation of enemy positions

REINFORCEMENTS—extra troops sent into battle

SABOTAGE—damage or destruction of property that is done on purpose

SOVIET UNION—Russia and 14 other now-independent countries

INTERNET SITES

Use FactHound to find Internet sites related to this book.

Visit www.facthound.com

Just type in 9780756556907 and go.

A Perspectives Flip Book

The Split History of the

D-Day Invasion

Allies' Perspective

By Michael Burgan

Content Consultant:
G. Kurt Piehler, PhD
Associate Professor of History
Director, Institute on World War and the Human Experience
Florida State University

COMPASS POINT BOOKS
a capstone imprint

Compass Point Books are published by Capstone,
1710 Roe Crest Drive, North Mankato, Minnesota 56003
www.mycapstone.com

LIBRARY OF CONGRESS CATALOGING-IN-PUBLICATION DATA IS AVAILABLE ON THE LIBRARY OF CONGRESS WEBSITE

ISBN 9780756556907 (libary binding)
ISBN 9780756568566 (paperback)
ISBN 9780756556983 (eBook PDF)

Summary: Every battle has two sides, and the D-Day Invasion during World War II is no different. Experience the event from perspective of the Allies, and then read the perspective of the Germans. A deeper understanding of the battle from both sides will give readers a clearer view of this historic event.

EDITOR
JENNIFER HUSTON

DESIGNER
HEIDI THOMPSON

MEDIA RESEARCHER
TRACY CUMMINS

PRODUCTION SPECIALIST
KATHY MCCOLLEY

IMAGE CREDITS

Allies' Perspective:

Capstone Press: Eric Gohl, 28; Defense Visual Information Center: NARA, Cover Top; Getty Images: Apic, 12, IWM/Sgt. Wilkes, 19, Time Life Pictures, 10, Universal History Archive/UIG, 23; Library of Congress Prints and Photographs Division: 16; Newscom: Everett Collection, Cover Bottom, NI Syndication, 5; Shutterstock: Everett Historical, 6, Keith Tarrier, 21, Olinchuk, 15; Wikimedia: NARA/T4c. Messerlin. (Army), 9

German Perspective:

Alamy: Maurice Savage, 13, MGPhoto76, 23; Defense Visual Information Center: NARA, Back Cover Bottom; Getty Images: AFP, 21, Galerie Bilderwelt, 11, Hulton Archive, 6, Mondadori Portfolio, 5, ullstein bild Dtl, 10, Universal History Archive, 17; Newscom: Everett Collection, Back Cover Top; Shutterstock: Vitek Prchal, 8

Printed and bound in the United States of America. PO3750

Table of Contents

Shared Resources

Chapter 1

Planning an Invasion

With a storm tossing the seas, a tiny British submarine came to the water's surface off the coast of Normandy, France. It was late evening on June 5, 1944, and the minisub's five-man crew was tuning its radio to receive a coded message. The sub, called *X23*, was so small that the men had to take turns sleeping in its two bunks. They also worried if the bottles of oxygen that helped keep them alive would last until they completed their mission. The sailors waited to hear if they were going to take part in the largest amphibious assault ever attempted.

The captain of an X-class minisub stands on deck giving orders to the crew just three weeks before the D-Day invasion. Minisubs played a key role in the attack.

The radio message came through; the attack was on. *X23* returned below the water's surface to avoid being detected by German ships or soldiers on land.

In the late 1930s, Germany had invaded large parts of Europe, including France. The amphibious assault planned for Normandy was designed to push the Germans out of the lands they had conquered and bring an end to World War II (1939–1945).

The crew of *X23* and another British minisub waited throughout the night. They had orders to surface again early on the morning of June 6. At that time, they would help guide British troops and tanks ashore, playing a key role in what the world knows today as D-Day.

A DREAM OF CONQUEST

World War II had started with Germany's invasion of Poland on September 1, 1939. German Chancellor Adolf Hitler had several goals in mind when he sent troops there and into other European countries. First, he wanted to make Germany the most powerful country in Europe. He also wanted to take back lands that Germany had been forced to give up after losing World War I (1914–1918). Hitler also wanted to rule over people who he considered inferior to Germans, such as the Poles. He believed Germans were superior to most other people and had a right to deny those people even their basic human rights. He particularly hated Jews, and anti-Semitism fueled many of his government's actions. Shortly after Hitler's Nazi Party came to power in Germany in 1933, they passed laws that limited the freedom of Germany's Jewish citizens. Some were sent to prisons called concentration camps. As he conquered countries

Prisoners at concentration camps were given very little to eat. Two men in front are holding up a friend who is too weak to stand on his own.

across Europe, Hitler sent millions of European Jews to these camps. Some of the camps were "death camps." By the time World War II ended, the Germans had killed more than 6 million Jews—two-thirds of the entire Jewish population in Europe at the time.

Hitler also imprisoned non-Jewish people across Europe. Some were his political opponents. Others were from religious groups he didn't like. And some were imprisoned simply because they were physically or mentally disabled.

Great Britain and France declared war on Germany on September 3, 1939. These and other nations that fought Germany were called the Allies. The Soviet Union joined the Allies in June 1941. Germany and the countries that supported it, including Italy and Japan, were known as the Axis Powers.

At first, the United States did not send troops to the war front. After World War I, many Americans did not want to take part in another European war. Congress even passed laws that limited when the United States could help other countries at war. However, President Franklin Roosevelt saw the danger Hitler posed to the people of Europe and their freedom. In 1940 he convinced Congress to give the Allies weapons and military supplies.

The war finally came to the United States on December 7, 1941. On that day, waves of Japanese planes attacked U.S. naval ships stationed at Pearl Harbor in Hawaii. The next day, the United States declared war on Japan. On December 11, Hitler declared war on the United States. In the blink of an eye, the United States had been pulled into the deadliest war the world had ever known.

SEEKING A SECOND FRONT

By the end of 1941, Germany had conquered 11 countries in Europe, including France, which had surrendered in June 1940. A year later Germany launched an invasion of the Soviet Union. The fighting between the Germans and Soviets affected large parts of Eastern Europe, and the Soviets suffered heavy losses. The fighting in the east became the major European battlefront.

Soviet Premier Joseph Stalin urged Roosevelt and British Prime Minister Winston Churchill to open a second battlefront in Europe. Since June 1941, the Soviets had been fighting the majority of the German Army. By the end of the war, their casualties were in the millions. Stalin suggested an invasion of France, which would force the Germans to move some of their troops out of the Soviet Union. Roosevelt was on board, but Churchill had another idea: In late 1942, he suggested that the Allies first attack German-controlled lands in North Africa. From there, the Allies could attack Italy. As that fighting went on, the Allies could then start making plans for the amphibious invasion of France. They went forward with this revised plan of attack, and the invasion in France was given the code name Operation Overlord. Today, it is known as D-Day, which is a term used to describe a day on which an important event is planned.

PREPARING FOR OVERLORD

The Allies chose U.S. General Dwight D. Eisenhower to command the troops that would invade France. He had helped train troops during World War I. In 1942 and 1943, he commanded

General Dwight Eisenhower commanded the troops at Normandy and later became president of the United States.

U.S. troops that fought in North Africa and Italy.

Eisenhower received orders from the Combined Chiefs of Staff in February 1944 which said, "You will enter the continent of Europe and . . . undertake operations aimed at . . . Germany and the destruction of her armed forces." By early 1944 Eisenhower had nearly 3 million troops under his command. About half were American. The rest were mostly British and Canadian.

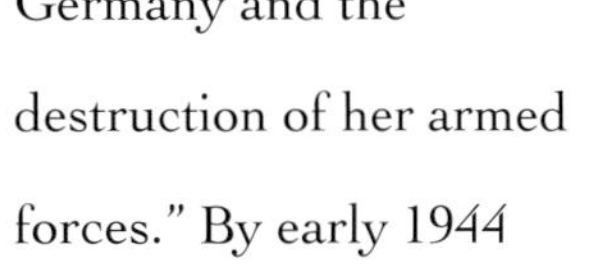

Leading up to D-Day, the Allies worked hard to deceive the Germans. They created fake plans for invading Norway, which Germany also controlled. They also wanted it to look like the attack would come at Pas-de-Calais, France, north of Normandy. The Allies sent out fake radio messages for the Germans to hear, describing an invasion force at Pas-de-Calais that didn't exist. They even built fake tanks and trucks out of rubber to trick German reconnaissance planes.

German spies who had been caught in England also helped the Allies. They agreed to work for the Allies rather than go to prison or be executed. These double agents helped spread false information about where the attack would occur and the size of the Allied forces.

ULTRA AND ENIGMA

The Allies had one way to measure how successful they were in deceiving the Germans. The Germans used a machine called Enigma to send coded messages, and the codes used changed daily. But in 1941 British mathematician Alan Turing was able to crack the code. Experts and an early computer helped Turing break Enigma's code and read the messages. The British called the information they gathered this way Ultra. By some estimates, cracking the Enigma code helped shorten the war by two years.

German soldiers used the Enigma machine to send coded messages.

Just before D-Day, the Allies learned the location of some underwater land mines the Germans had planted. With this information, the Allies could tell that the Germans believed the false information they had sent out.

During the buildup for Operation Overlord, the Allies kept their real intentions a secret. They built new airfields across England to use for the invasion. They hid supplies of ammunition in remote areas and brought in thousands of tanks and other vehicles. By May 1944 Eisenhower had decided the attack would come in June. He later wrote that the troops gathered in England were as "tense as a coiled spring . . . a great human spring coiled for the moment when its energy should be released."

CHAPTER 2

APPROACHING D-DAY

Eisenhower did not pick the date for Operation Overlord by chance. Weather, the tides, and the phases of the moon all played a part in the decision. Originally, the operation was planned for May, which would give the Allies more time to carry out their invasion during the warm summer months. Plus, Eisenhower knew that the Germans were building up their defenses along the Atlantic Coast in France to try to stop an amphibious invasion. Launching the attack in May would give them less time to do so.

However, Eisenhower decided to wait until June because he needed more time to build up the largest force possible for the attack. He decided the attack would come between June 5 and June 7. Those three days offered the best combination of a late-rising full moon and low tides. The late-rising full moon would give the first wave of troops more time to operate under darkness. The low tide would help the small landing craft carrying troops ashore avoid any obstacles the Germans had placed near the coast.

ALLIED ADVANTAGES

The switch from May to June also gave the Allies more time to use one of their huge military advantages—air power. In the weeks leading up to D-Day, bombers targeted German coastal defenses and artillery. They also destroyed bridges, railways, and trains so the Germans would have a hard time bringing reinforcements and supplies to Normandy.

By June 1 Allied bombing raids had destroyed almost all the bridges across the Seine, the major river that flows through northern France.

Members of the French Resistance set off explosives to destroy railroad tracks and sabotage the Nazis.

The Allies relied on help from the French Resistance—citizens who covertly operated against the Germans in support of the Allies by gathering information and carrying out sabotage. The Resistance cut telephone lines, which hindered communication for the Germans. Along railroad tracks the Resistance placed explosives, which they would set off when they received word of the invasion. A secret code sent by radio would alert them when the attack was about to begin.

The Jedburghs

Both the British and Americans had organizations to spy and carry out secret missions behind enemy lines. For the British, the Special Operations Executive (SOE) did this work. For the Americans, it was the Office of Strategic Services (OSS). Together, members of the SOE and OSS worked with the French Resistance as part of special units called the Jedburghs. Each team usually included one British, American, and French member. On the night of June 5, the Jedburghs began parachuting into France and carried out sabotage to prevent the Germans from bringing reinforcements to Normandy, which aided the Allies in their ultimate victory on D-Day.

MAKING THE DECISION

With the information he had, Eisenhower chose June 5 for Operation Overlord. But ultimately, the weather would determine the day of the attack. If none of those days in early June worked, they would have to wait several weeks for the conditions they

wanted. But a delay could be disastrous. If the Allies waited, the Germans could learn of the attack, and the element of surprise would be lost. Also, the Germans could strengthen their defenses and build new weapons. Waiting was not an option.

On June 4, Eisenhower and his staff met with chief meteorologist, Captain James Stagg. But Stagg didn't have good news. A storm was about to hit the coast of Normandy with strong winds and high waves that would make it difficult for the landing craft to safely reach shore. After some debate, Eisenhower decided to postpone the mission. Operation Overlord, or D-Day, would take place on June 6, weather permitting.

Early on the morning of June 5, Eisenhower once again met with his aides and Stagg. The meteorologist thought the weather would break long enough to launch the invasion the following day. Eisenhower decided it was worth the risk.

Some vessels, like the minisubs *X20* and *X23*, were already at sea. The men who would take part in the first wave of the assault got ready to join them. Between the airborne troops and those landing on shore, the Allies had a force of 156,000 men prepared to fight the Germans in Normandy. The Allies also had more than 7,000 ships and boats of all sizes ready for the invasion, along with almost 15,000 aircraft and gliders. Joining the U.S., British, and Canadian forces were troops from Australia, Belgium, Czechoslovakia, France, Greece, the Netherlands, New Zealand, Norway, and Poland.

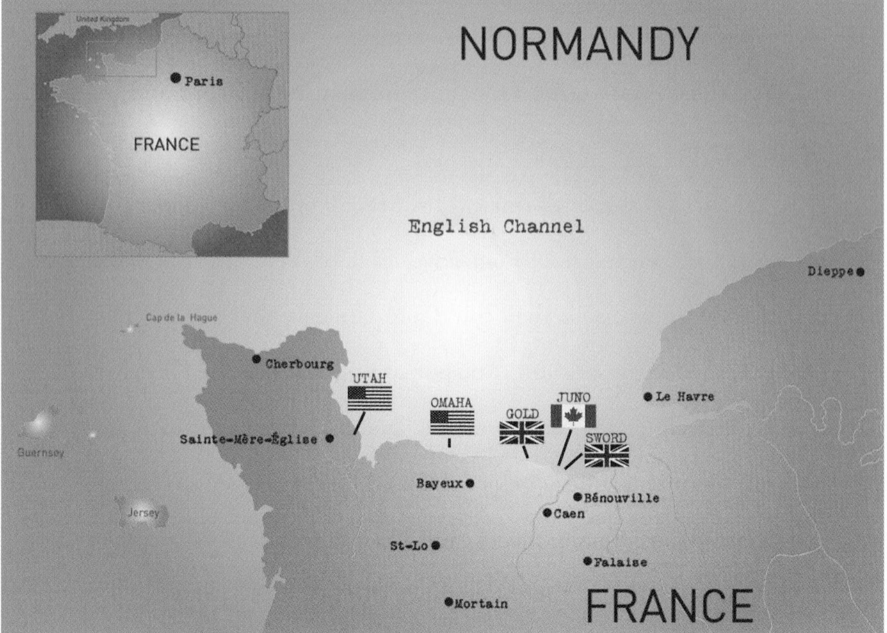

LAST-MINUTE PREPARATIONS

During the day on June 5, ships filled with soldiers began leaving their docks and heading across the English Channel. Once on the water, the seas were choppy, and many of the men got seasick. On a British ship, William Seymour saw "waves coming over the side of the ship. . . . But on we went, rocking from side to side." Despite the rough crossing, many of the men knew they had a mission to do. Alfred Leonard, a 16-year-old member of the Merchant Navy, later said, "You were very aware that what was about to happen was going to be important."

As they neared France, the men boarded smaller landing craft. Then, they waded ashore at five beaches stretching 45 miles (72 kilometers) along the Normandy coast. Each beach had its

own code name. The Americans were headed to Omaha and Utah beaches, the Canadians to Juno, and the British to Sword and Gold beaches.

While the ships moved toward France, 20,000 paratroopers prepared for their mission. Planes would take them past the German defenses on the shore so they could parachute farther inland. Their goal was to block important transportation routes so the Germans could not easily send reinforcements. Bomber crews got ready to take out German artillery before the land forces arrived. The huge operation required many pieces, and Eisenhower knew that the invasion could fail. On the night of June 5, he met some U.S. paratroopers just before they boarded their aircraft. He watched them take off for France and then went back to his camp. The outcome of D-Day was out of his control.

General Eisenhower has some encouraging words for Allied paratroopers before they leave to parachute into France.

Chapter 3

Invading Normandy

Just after midnight on June 6, as the troops on the ships prepared to storm the beaches of Normandy, 180 British commandos were already at work in France. Flying in six lightweight glider planes, they had quietly landed near the town of Bénouville. Their mission was to capture and hold two bridges in the region. British land forces would need to use those bridges once they came ashore.

With the element of surprise, the commandos quickly overwhelmed the bridges' defenders. In less than 20 minutes, the commandos had accomplished their mission.

Meanwhile, the first paratroopers began landing around the region. They carried packs weighing up to 100 pounds (45 kilograms) that were filled with weapons and supplies. But the landings didn't always go smoothly. Some paratroopers missed their targets. Others landed in trees and frantically cut off their parachutes before they could be captured by the Germans. In addition, the Germans had flooded some fields with water to make it difficult for the Allies to carry out an invasion. Under the weight of their heavy packs, some of the paratroopers drowned.

The thousands of paratroopers who landed safely began attacking German positions. American paratroopers were supposed to land outside the town of Sainte-Mère-Église, but some landed in the center of it and were quickly gunned down by the Germans. Others came upon French residents living near the town. Marcelle Hamel-Hateau saw a paratrooper land outside her house. He told her, "It's the big invasion . . . thousands of paratroopers are landing in this countryside tonight." Across Normandy, French residents like Hamel-Hateau welcomed the Allies' arrival.

APPROACHING THE BEACHES

Throughout the morning, Allied landing craft headed for the five target beaches. Meanwhile, more than 7,500 tons of bombs were dropped on German defensive positions along the coast. Some of

the bombers also hit targets farther inland. The German air force had few planes in the region, so the Allied bombers flew with little resistance from German fighter planes.

British troops headed to Sword Beach on D-Day.

The men in the landing craft watched as the Allied bombs sent dirt and smoke into the air. They counted on the planes to weaken the German defenses before their landing craft hit the beaches. Allied ships also fired their guns at the Germans waiting on shore. Author Ernest Hemingway was on one of the landing craft. He described how the boom of the giant naval guns shook the soldiers' helmets. The sound "struck your . . . ear like a punch with a heavy, dry glove."

In addition to troops, the British were also bringing ashore some amphibious tanks that could advance through shallow water as well as roll on land. They also had tanks called "funnies" that were designed to carry out special duties. Some shot flames almost 400 feet (122 m). Others had revolving barrels in the front that could explode land mines the Germans had buried in the sand.

The Germans had also placed land mines and obstacles in the water. Huge steel frames called Belgian gates formed a wall off the coast. Other obstacles, called hedgehogs, had crossed steel beams up to 5 feet (1.5 m) tall. Some obstacles also had land mines attached to them. Specially trained teams of sailors had the job of

blowing up the obstacles before the landing craft reached them. Along with U.S. Army engineers, they were supposed to clear paths 50 feet (15 m) wide. These sailors were nicknamed "frogmen" because they originally wore green rubber suits in the water.

As the Allied landing craft approached the beaches, the Germans on shore began firing back. The frogmen worked as bullets whizzed by their heads. Meanwhile, some landing craft were tossed by the rough seas into obstacles and land mines that hadn't been destroyed. Some troops landed in the water without their weapons and tried to swim ashore as the Germans fired at them. Along the five beaches, the Allied troops began to realize that the bombing raids and naval guns had not destroyed as much of the German defenses as Eisenhower had hoped.

ACTION ON THE BEACHES

At 6:30 a.m. the first troops came ashore at Omaha and Utah beaches. Additional troops began hitting the other three beaches soon after. Some men drowned in the rough waters before they could reach the shore. Others were hit by German gunfire. Medics came to the aid of the wounded and dying who screamed for help.

Meanwhile, additional U.S. soldiers kept pouring out of the landing craft. Once on shore, they tried to take cover behind obstacles or small rocks. Some dodged minefields to approach the German defenses. Their goal was to get close enough to toss hand grenades inside and take out the Germans manning the machine guns. But enemy gunfire was also coming from the cliffs above the

beaches. U.S. naval ships moved closer to shore to try to knock out the German defenses, while thousands of men continued to storm the beaches. As one U.S. infantry unit reported, "The enemy now began to pour artillery and mortar fire on to the [crowded] beach with deadly precision and effect." The fighting at Omaha Beach was the bloodiest of the day, with an estimated 3,686 casualties compared to 4,158 at the other four beaches combined.

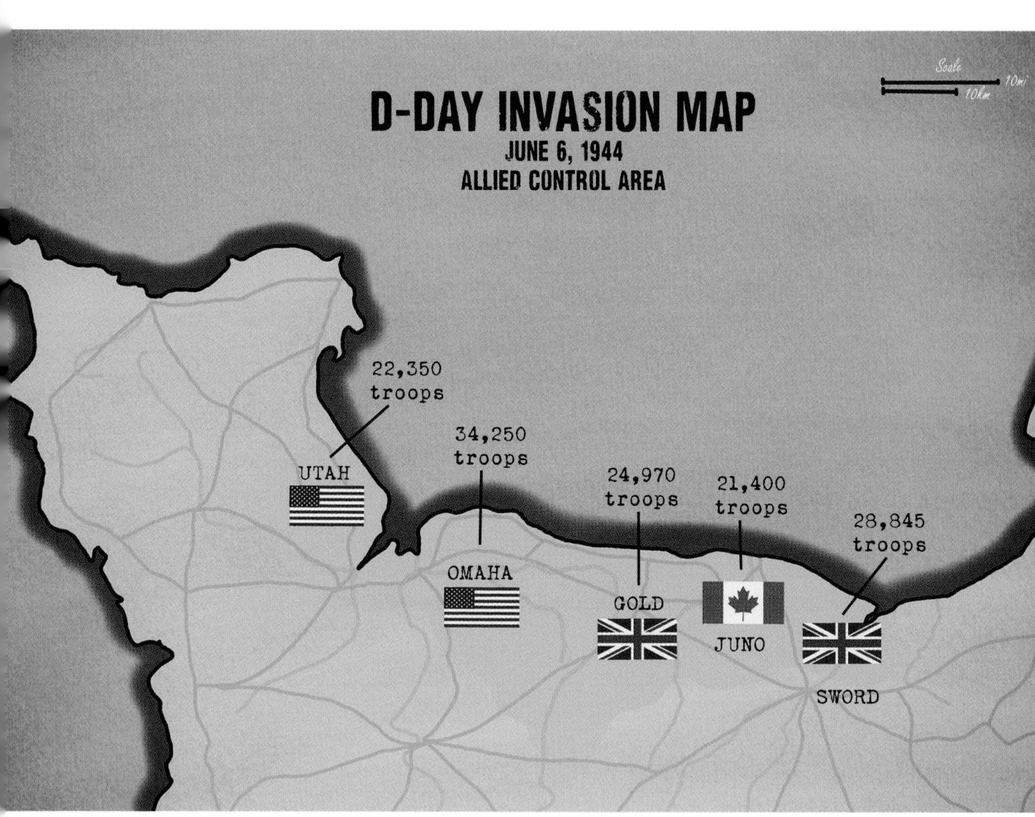

The beaches where the Allies landed on D-Day spanned a 45-mile (72-km) stretch.

The landing at Utah Beach started poorly with the troops missing their planned target, but the mistake turned into an advantage. German defenses were lighter there than at the planned landing spot, so the American troops quickly came ashore. At Omaha Beach, the rough water had sank most of the amphibious tanks before they reached shore, but more of them made it at Utah Beach. The coast there also had fewer obstacles. The next waves of incoming troops headed for the same spot rather than the original target. They came ashore with little German resistance.

The British and Canadians had an easier time landing on the beaches than the Americans. Still, at times they faced fierce fighting. At Gold Beach, British troops battled all day to establish a firm position on the beach. British soldier Ken Coney, who came ashore that morning, later wrote in his diary, "Dead and dying are everywhere. I can't understand why I am not frightened." At Sword Beach, British and French troops needed less than an hour to move inland and reach their first target.

BACK IN ENGLAND

As the fighting raged throughout the morning, Eisenhower waited for news. He had already written a message he would send to the world if the invasion failed. It said in part, "If any blame or fault attaches to the attempt, it is mine alone." But as the attack went on, he was pleased with the reports he heard. At 10 a.m. the British Broadcasting Company (BBC) played a message that Eisenhower had recorded earlier. It began, "People of Western

D-Day was an enormous undertaking that involved 156,000 Allied troops, 7,000 ships and landing craft, 11,000 aircraft, and 13,000 paratroopers.

Europe: a landing was made this morning on the coast of France. . . . This landing is part of the . . . United Nations plan for the liberation of Europe, made [together] with our great Russian allies. I have this message for all of you. Although the initial assault may not have been made in your own country, the hour of your liberation is approaching."

However, by the end of the day, the Allies had not met all of their goals. The British and Canadian forces had not taken the town of Bayeux or the city of Caen as Eisenhower and his staff had hoped. And there were still gaps along the beaches between the various Allied forces. But the Allies had managed to bring more than 150,000 men ashore. Ultimately, D-Day was a success for the Allies, but the fighting was far from over.

A REAL PRIVATE RYAN

The 1998 movie *Saving Private Ryan* shows the death and destruction of D-Day in gruesome detail. The movie also tells the story of a group of U.S. soldiers who take on a dangerous mission behind German lines. They're sent to find and bring home a paratrooper after his brothers were killed in battle.

The plot is similar to a real-life story that occurred after D-Day. Frederick "Fritz" Niland was one of four brothers who served during World War II. Fritz took part in the Normandy invasion, but in July, he was ordered home because his three brothers were believed to have been killed in battle. (One was actually in a Japanese prisoner-of-war camp and later managed to escape.) President Roosevelt had earlier said that no American family should lose more than two sons during the war. When Niland heard he was going to be sent home, at first he refused, but he eventually followed orders and returned home.

Chapter 4

After D-Day

On June 7, General Eisenhower talked with his generals in Normandy. Although the Allies had successfully landed on all five beaches, some German forces remained in the area and continued to fire artillery at the Allies.

While the first Allied troops to land on Normandy pushed inland, more came ashore. The goal was to link the five beachheads into one solid line of Allied troops and weapons. That would prevent the Germans from trying to attack through any gaps in the line. Then the Allies could safely bring ashore all the supplies and weapons they would need to push their way into the heart of France.

THE FIGHTING GOES ON

The number of Allied casualties on D-Day is hard to pin down, but historians place it around 11,000. This includes an estimated 4,400 Allied troops killed on the beaches during the invasion. Also included in the number of casualties are those who were taken prisoner—mostly paratroopers or pilots whose planes were shot down. The number of casualties continued to grow in the weeks that followed, but the Allies managed to gain more ground.

The Germans put up a stiff defense around Caen, and their reinforcements began to arrive from other parts of France. The Germans also used planes to drop land mines off the coast to slow the Allies' efforts to bring in more men and supplies. Specially designed Allied ships "swept" the waters of the land mines.

Eisenhower called these first few weeks of fighting in Normandy "the Battle of the Beachhead." The Allies gained ground slowly, but as Eisenhower later wrote, "It was during this period that the stage was set for the later, spectacular liberation of France and Belgium." During this time, the Allies began moving ashore more than 2 million troops that would carry out that liberation.

The Allies maintained their superior air power, which made it difficult for the Germans to move reinforcements to the front. The Allies also continued to rely on the French Resistance and Jedburgh teams to sabotage and slow down the Germans. And in the first days after D-Day, the Allies kept sending fake messages to deceive the Germans. Those messages convinced Hitler and some of his generals that another attack was still to come.

By the end of July, the British and Canadians had driven the Germans out of Caen. The fighting there was particularly heavy, with several hundred Allied tanks destroyed. Even so, the Allied invasion of France was under way with a goal to not just push back the Germans but also close in on them and destroy as much of their army as possible.

The Germans launched counterattacks when they could, including one in early August near Mortain. Against U.S. forces led by General George Patton, the Germans initially advanced, but they were soon pushed back. The Allies then circled the German troops near Falaise, killing about 10,000 and capturing 50,000 others.

THE SECOND INVASION

As the fighting went on around Mortain and Falaise, the Allies launched a second amphibious assault on France. On August 15, they came ashore on the Mediterranean coast in the south of France. As at Normandy, they relied on paratroopers, planes, and naval guns to begin the attack. German defenses were much weaker in southern France than they had been at Normandy. French forces quickly took control of the port city of Marseille, and U.S. troops headed north along the Rhône River. By September, the Americans united with Allied forces pushing east from Normandy, and together they advanced toward the German border.

By then, the Allies had liberated Paris from the Germans. For more than four years, the city's residents had been under German rule. In late August, as the Allies approached the city,

the German troops surrendered. Soon, a million joyful Parisians filled the streets to welcome the Allies.

Throughout the rest of 1944 and into the spring of 1945, the Allies continued their push eastward toward Germany. But there were some setbacks along the way. A September operation in the Netherlands called Market Garden ended in failure. British and American paratroopers were supposed to take several bridges across the Rhine River to make it easier for ground forces to invade Germany. However, the Germans had experienced troops in the area, and they held off the attack. Then, in December, the Germans launched their last great counterattack, known as the Battle of the Bulge. During the fighting in the forests of Belgium, the Germans inflicted heavy losses on the Allies, but they also lost 80,000 men in the process. All this went on as Soviet troops continued to fight German forces in Eastern Europe.

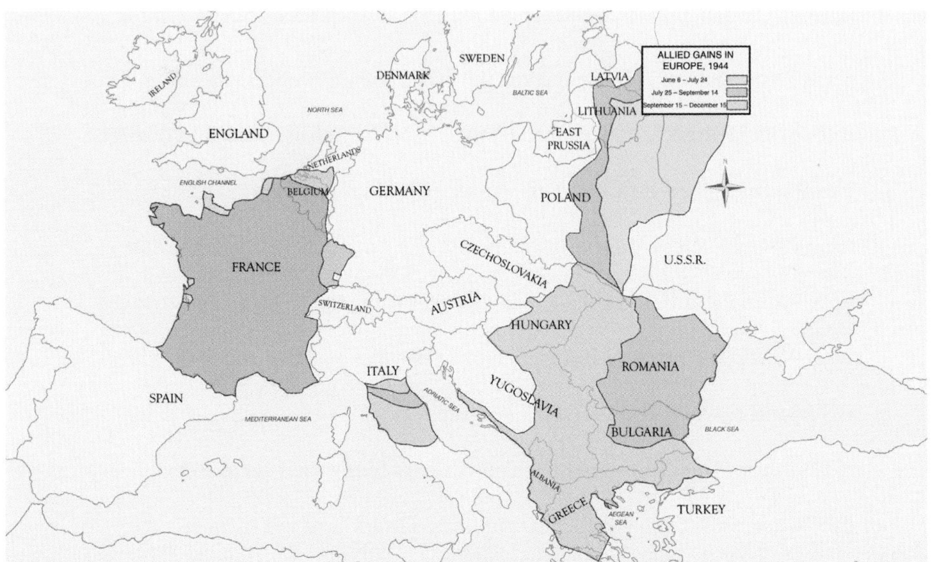

D-Day was a turning point for the Allies in World War II. After the invasion, the Allies took back much of the land that the Nazis had taken over.

The spring of 1945 saw the Allies moving toward the German capital of Berlin from two sides. The Soviets advanced from the east, while the British and American forces came from the west. The Soviets reached Berlin first and began bombarding the city on April 20, Hitler's birthday. Ten days later, Hitler committed suicide, and on May 8, Germany officially surrendered. Although fighting continued in some parts of Europe and Asia, the war against the Nazis was over.

FINAL VICTORY

After D-Day, it took the Allies less than a year to defeat Nazi Germany. Without the successful landing at Normandy, the Allies could not have amassed the huge force they needed to push back the Germans. Eisenhower believed the Allies' superior air power and the Germans' lack of good intelligence about what the Allies planned to do were largely responsible for achieving this goal.

In writing his report on the fighting in Europe, Eisenhower also noted the important role civilians played in producing all the weapons and equipment the troops used. He wrote, "No army or navy was ever supported so generously or so well. Never . . . were we forced to fight a major battle without the weapons that were needed."

Although the massive D-Day invasion took place decades ago, the world still remembers the bravery and courage the troops showed in one of the most important battles in world history.

INDEX